Ephesians KJV Bible Commentary

James Battell

Published by James Battell, 2024.

EPHESIANS KJV BIBLE COMMENTARY

First edition. February 2, 2024.

ISBN: 979-8224974184

Written by James Battell.

Also by James Battell

The Shocking History of the Jesuits (The Society of Jesus)

King James I of England: The King The Vatican Could Not Kill

The Hidden Truth About Freemasonry, The Catholic Church, And The Illuminati

Bible Prophecy Made Simple For Serious Students of Scripture

Did The Catholic Church Order Abraham Lincoln's Assassination?

Is Calvinism and the Doctrines of Grace Biblical?

The Book of Genesis Commentary (Chapters 1-11)

The Book of Genesis Commentary (Chapters 1-11)

Watchman Nee, Witness Lee, and Living Stream Ministry: A Critical Analysis of Their Identity as Cult or Church

What Is Speaking In Tongues And Is It Still For Today?

Ephesians KJV Bible Commentary

The Book of Romans Commentary

Philemon Bible Study (Slavery In Scripture)

Turbulent Thrones: Charles vs. Cromwell's Epic Struggle for England's Soul

The Holy Ghost Within The Trinity

Papal Infallibility or Insanity?

The Immaculate Conception ("Deception")

Table of Contents

The way I approach a book in the Bible to study it is to read it again and again over several days and have mental notes, of course. But when it comes to recording, I literally just sit down (and this time I did sit down: I no longer stand, I sit) and I sit down and I just read the verses and I give you the first thoughts that comes to my mind. I have no notes. So, it's a very unique way of doing things, not necessarily very scholarly. But, I'm not a scholar. I'm just an ordinary, self-taught, born-again Bible-believing Christian. Saved nearly 13 years, I might add.

But Ephesians chapter 1 starts with Paul (almost like a forensic lawyer would do) arguing so articulately how we are already in Christ in Heaven, dealing with predestination, which occurred before the foundation of the world. But let's read these verses and see what he says.

Verse 3: "Blessed *be* the God and Father of our Lord Jesus Christ, who hath blessed us with all spiritual blessings in heavenly *places* in Christ: According as he hath chosen us in him before the foundation of the world, that we should be holy and without blame before him in love". That's dealing with one's predestination, not justification, not sanctification.

And he goes on in verse 5: "Having predestinated us unto the adoption of children by Jesus Christ to himself, according to the good pleasure of his will, To the praise of the glory of his grace, wherein he hath made us accepted in the beloved." Incredible!

But you've got to remember one thing: that nobody was in Christ *per se* before the foundation of the world, because nobody existed before the foundation of the world.

These verses are dealing with the mind of Christ through God's foreknowledge. He's predestinated us, the Church, those which would appropriate the atonement to be in Christ, found holy and without blame before Him in love. You see, Paul bypasses justification and sanctification and he goes right down to the nitty-gritty. He's looking at one's adoption, which is what this is all about.

We are to be adopted into the family of God and from Galatians 3, there's neither Jew nor Gentile any longer. And he says it's already happened (from verse 3). He's already blessed us with all spiritual blessings in heavenly places, which means, spiritually speaking, we're not only in Christ ("once saved, always saved" or "if saved, always saved"), but we are already in heaven in a spiritual sense.

And he goes on to say in verse 7: "In whom we have redemption [complete forgiveness] through his blood [Jesus Christ, of course], the forgiveness of sins, according to the riches of his grace; Wherein he hath abounded toward us in all wisdom and prudence". By His precious blood we are saved from all of our past, present and future sins. Amen!

But look at verse 12: "That we should be to the praise of his glory, who first trusted in Christ." To believe, to receive, to trust is all synonymous. See, Paul starts his epistle from chapter 1 looking at our predestination, which occurred through the foreknowledge of the Lord before the foundation of the world. But by verse 12, he says that "That we should be to the praise of his glory, who first trusted in Christ."

You see, you have to hear the gospel ("faith cometh by hearing, and hearing by the word of God", Romans 10:17). And once you've heard it and believed it and trusted in Him, then you are predestinated to be conformed to the image of Christ.

How you marry up the two – the Lord's sovereignty and man's free will – I think, is impossible to do. It's like the tri-unity of God. You weren't told to understand it, but you were told to believe it.

But look at verse 13: "In whom ye also *trusted*, after that ye heard the word of truth, the gospel of your salvation: in whom also after that ye believed, ye were sealed with that holy Spirit of promise." The Holy Ghost has sealed you unto the day of redemption, which for us would be the Judgment Seat of Christ. It's like tightly sealing a jar shut. Only the person who sealed it shut can unseal it. So, only God can unseal those that He has sealed into the body of the Christ.

You see, not only have you been put into Christ Jesus through a spiritual baptism (not through a water baptism), but you are now kept in Him. You're sealed. And chapter 4, verse 30, cross-references this. So, you're in Christ Jesus. And not only are you in Him, but the triune God is in you, as well.

So, those opening comments will, I guess, deal with chapter 1. And like I say, Paul is a master when it comes to dealing with the Lord's sovereignty and man's free will (and yes, they do both go side-by-side). To suggest otherwise is doing the Scripture a injustice.

You see, the way this works is quite simply this: the Lord God of the Bible has provided an atonement for the sins of the whole world. That's called provision. But you and I and all of us have to personally appropriate the atonement for it to be relevant to us.

So, while he starts his epistle dealing with us already being Heaven (which is incredible to even try to fathom), he then has to deal with us living in time, from verse 12 and 13, how we have to hear the gospel, to believe it, to receive it.

Let's move on. Chapter 2, verse 1: "And you *hath he quickened*, who were dead in trespasses and sins". That simply means that you were unregenerated before you became regenerated. You cannot get total inability or total depravity from chapter 2, verse one. Your spirit was dead so you need God to bring it alive. This is the new birth.

And I did a study some months ago going through Luke's Gospel where I dealt with the prodigal son who was dead and it says "he came to himself". And when he came himself, he was reconciled unto his father.

And there's two arguments or two views on that piece of Scripture. Some people say, well, he was saved but backslid. Others say, no, he wasn't saved until he came to himself. Well, either way, he came to himself. Nothing in the text says that God did anything for him or to him to bring him to himself.

Now I will say this. We know from Acts 5 that God has granted repentance to the Jews. That's one group of people. We know from Acts 11 how God has granted repentance to the Gentiles. That's another group of people. And that's all there is in the world: either Jew or Gentile. But once you're born-again, you are in the Church. There is now neither Jew nor Gentile, just the Christian.

We know from John 12 how the Lord Jesus Christ has drawn all men unto Himself. We know from 2 Corinthians 5:19, that "God was in Christ, reconciling the world unto himself", and we know from 2 Corinthians 6:2: "now *is* the day of salvation".

And Paul says in the latter verses of 2 Corinthians 5:20: "be ye reconciled to God". So, if you come across someone who says: "Hey, look at me, aren't I a wonderful person? A super holy person. I'm born-again. You know, I believe in the Lord Jesus

Christ. Blah, blah, blah." Yes, you did because He granted you repentance and He drew you unto Himself. "For the Son of man is come to seek and to save that which was lost" (Luke 19:10).

What else have we got here?

Continue on through Ephesians chapter 2. Look at verse 6: "And hath raised *us* up together, and made *us* sit together in heavenly *places* in Christ Jesus". That's almost a continuation of our spiritual standing. We are already in the heavenly places, the third heaven, of course. Now we are seated and reigning with the King. Amen!

I remember telling this to a charismatic, who nearly had a fit because they don't think you can know you are saved and they think you can lose your salvation. How can you lose your salvation when you're already in Heaven? In fact, I'll give you a cross-reference to this: John 5:24, Jesus speaking: "Verily, verily, I say unto you, He that heareth my word, and believeth on him that sent me, <u>hath</u> everlasting life, and shall <u>not</u> come into condemnation; but is passed from death unto <u>life</u>." You're already judgment free; you've passed from death unto life. You're ruling with the Lord in heavenly places right now.

I'll give you one more Scripture: Colossians chapter 3, verse 1: "If ye then be risen with Christ, seek those things which are above, where Christ sitteth on the right hand of God." You see, you're not only saved from all of your past, present and future sins, you're not only in the hand of the Father and of the Son, but your spirit (if you're born again) is in the heavenly places in Christ Jesus.

Ephesians 2, verse 8 (you know this so very well): "For by grace are ye saved through faith; and that not of yourselves: *it is* the gift of God: Not of works, lest any man should boast." This has to be one of the clearest Scriptures concerning one's salvation being a free gift.

Look at verse 10: "For we are his workmanship, created in Christ Jesus unto good works, which God hath before ordained that we should walk in them." You take Ephesians 2, you take James 2, and the two harmonise beautifully. Paul's dealing with one's justification in the sight of God, whereas James is dealing with one's justification in the sight of man. And if you're saved, your good works will follow you, and mankind will see your works and he will know that you belong to the Lord Jesus Christ. But your good works do not prove you are saved and neither are they automatic because you can refuse to do them when you backslide.

Also from Ephesians 2:15: "Having abolished in his flesh the enmity, *even* the law of commandments *contained* in ordinances; for to make in himself of twain one new man, *so* making peace." He's abolished/fulfilled the law. We know that from Matthew 5:17. We are now under grace, which is a new covenant, not the law which is the old covenant.

Chapter 3, verse 9: "And to make all *men* see what *is* the fellowship of the mystery, which from the beginning of the world hath been hid in God, who created all things by Jesus Christ". He also (the Lord Jesus Christ) created the world, as did the Holy Spirit, from Job 26. God made everything by Jesus Christ and the Holy Spirit for Jesus Christ (Revelation chapter 4).

Ephesians chapter 4, verse 4: "*There is* one body, and one Spirit, even as ye are called in one hope of your calling; One Lord, one faith, one baptism, One God and Father of all, who *is* above all, and through all, and in you all." One Lord God, one true eternal God. Any other god is a false god. One faith (Biblical Christianity), one baptism (spiritual, not water) and God the Father is in you all (verse 6). Incredible!

Yes, there are many denominations and there are groups within groups which worship the Lord Jesus Christ, but if you're born again, you are in the Body of Christ. And He allows people to worship Him in different ways on different days of the week, as long as you are born again. That's the main thing.

Chapter 4, verse 19: "Who being past feeling have given themselves over unto lasciviousness, to work all uncleanness with greediness." When an unsaved man or woman arrives in Hell, they have only have themselves to blame. And Paul says it very clear here that these people have given themselves over to lasciviousness (all illicit sexual sins). And once that happens, according to Romans chapter 1, God then gives you over to a reprobate mind and you are finished!

Chapter 5 deals with submitting to one other, not even speaking of those things which are done in secret from verse 12, which always reminds me of the Freemasons, who meet and worship their god in secret.

And then by chapter 6, he says: "Children, obey your parents". The previous chapter dealt with husbands and wives which are saved submitting to one another, and our children are told to submit to their parents, in reference to saved parents. And the reason for this is very simple, because Paul wants to keep the family together. The family unit has never been under so much threat as it currently is. Not only can children divorce their parents today, but children can have abortions without their parents knowing and some children can even have sex changes. We are living in very dark times!

But he says here, from Ephesians 6, verse 16: "Above all, taking the shield of faith, wherewith ye shall be able to quench all the fiery darts of the wicked," in reference to Satan, of course. And he won't just come at you in a physical way. I mean, he could do, but he's more likely to come at you through your family: saved family members, unsaved family members. He may even come at you through carnal Christians, believe it or not! And he can come to you, or come at you, through depressions, disillusionment, job worries, marriage uncertainties, mortgage concerns.

That's why it says in chapter 5 for wives to submit to their husbands, and children to submit to their parents, because Satan will come at you through your children or through your spouses. If you're not married, if you're a sister in the Lord, and you're not married, you need some kind of covering, and it would come probably from a local church maybe, if you're in a church, from the brothers in that church. Or if you haven't got a church, maybe you have a brother in the Lord who's close to you. He's your covering because Satan will come at you as best as he can.

But like I say, depressions, disillusionment, job worries, marriage uncertainties, mortgage concerns also cause great worry and concern for children.

So I think these are the main points I wanted to cover as an introduction to the Epistle to the Ephesians. Six chapters and I'm very pleased I was able to record it rather quickly. The editing took a lot longer, of course. It always does.

But as far as I'm concerned, Paul was a genius. He was able to deal with the Lord's sovereignty through foreknowledge. Those that had appropriated the atonement had been predestinated to be adopted to be the children of God. But we have to believe on

Him, we have to receive Him, we have to trust on Him (chapter 1 verse 12) in order for that process to occur literally in our lifetimes.

Like I say, how you marry up the two – the Lord's sovereignty and man's free will – is beyond me. I don't really understand it, but I was told to believe it. It's like the tri-unity of God, you know, how you can believe that, or how you are expected to understand how one God has existed in three distinct Persons for all of eternity, is beyond me. But it's a Biblical fact, nonetheless.

So, I think these verses and this visual introduction to the Epistle to the Ephesians will hopefully whet your appetites when it comes to digging deep into the word of God, and we also know from Romans 12 how we are to present our bodies and minds daily as living sacrifices unto God, which is our reasonable service.

But I love chapter 4, verse 5: "One Lord, one faith, one baptism". Many groups within groups, like I say. But there's only one Lord: the triune God. Only one faith: Biblical Christianity. One baptism: spiritual, not water. "One God and Father of all, who *is* above all, and through all, and in you all." Only if (chapter 1, verse 12) you have trusted in Christ. Only if you have appropriated the atonement.

And I think that's about all I want to say for this visual intro to Ephesians. Ephesians runs to just over 80 pages. So, Lord willing, it will be a blessing to the brethren.

Chapter 5:16: "Redeeming the time, because the days are evil." (Sometimes a verse just slips through your mind.) And that's what we need to do as Bible-believing Christians. The days are evil (plural) but if we can redeem the time (buy it back), if we can reach out to the lost and we can encourage one another through books, such as this, or through any form, we should do so.

So, there you are. A brief and unique video intro. It's still very misty I can see, through my viewfinder, but it's been a great blessing to do Ephesians and I hope it blesses you, if you get a chance to listen to it. The Lord bless you all!

CHAPTER 1

VERSES 1-2: "Paul, an apostle of Jesus Christ by the will of God, to the saints which are at Ephesus, and to the faithful in Christ Jesus: Grace *be* to you, and peace, from God our Father, and *from* the Lord Jesus Christ."

This is a typical Pauline Epistle. It starts right at the beginning with his own Christian name. And Paul was made an apostle (verse 1) by the will of God. No man chose Paul to be an apostle. No synod laid their hands on Paul to be an apostle. He was chosen by Jesus Christ, according to Acts chapter 9.

Paul was not chosen before the foundation of the world. He was chosen post-Pentecost (Acts chapter 9). The saints found in verse 1 are those in Ephesus, which would consist of all born-again Bible-believing Christians. And the "faithful in Christ Jesus" would be another term to describe those that were born again.

"Grace *be* to you, and peace, from God our Father and *from* the Lord Jesus Christ." The term "grace" is one of the most used Pauline expressions in the New Testament.

Mankind deserves to go to Hell when it dies, but due to God being a loving and merciful Creator and Saviour and Redeemer, He's made it possible for the world to be saved through the death, burial and resurrection of the Lord Jesus Christ. Verse 1: You're <u>in</u> Christ Jesus, in reference to your eternal security, and also <u>in</u> reference to your eternal standing. "Once saved, always saved" or "if saved, always saved".

VERSES 3-6: "Blessed *be* the God and Father of our Lord Jesus Christ, who hath blessed us with all spiritual blessings

in heavenly *places* in Christ: According as he hath chosen us in him before the foundation of the world, that we should be holy and without blame before him in love: Having predestinated us unto the adoption of children by Jesus Christ to himself, according to the good pleasure of his will, To the praise of the glory of his grace, wherein he hath made us accepted in the beloved."

Verses 3 down to 6 are quoted nearly every time by Calvinists, when it comes to their understanding of how a person gets saved. They would have you believe that God has chosen person A, B and C before the foundation of the world to be saved, based primarily on God's good pleasure. But the Bible tells us that God is no respecter of persons. "For all have sinned and come short of the glory of God" (Romans 3:23).

And man, in his best possible state, is altogether vanity. Jesus Christ told us that nobody is good except God. So, what do these verses mean? Verse 3: "Blessed *be* the God and Father of our Lord Jesus Christ, who hath blessed us with all spiritual blessings in heavenly *places* in Christ". Past tense, of course. Heavenly places would be the third heaven. And He's given us all spiritual blessings.

The same language is found in 1 Corinthians chapter 1, from verse 5: "That in every thing ye are enriched by him, in all utterance, and *in* all knowledge; Even as the testimony of Christ was confirmed in you: So that ye come behind in no gift; waiting for the coming of our Lord Jesus Christ: Who shall also confirm you unto the end, *that ye may be* blameless in the day of our Lord Jesus Christ."

So, you are enriched by him in all utterance and in all knowledge. So, if you are born again you are as complete as you will ever be on this side of Heaven. But Paul goes on to say from Ephesians chapter 1, verse 4: "According as he hath chosen us in him before the foundation of the world [past tense, of course], that we [the saints from verse 1 and the faithful from verse 1] should be holy and without blame before him in love".

This is not in reference to a person's justification. This is in reference to a person's adoption, which comes after justification and sanctification. And verse 5 makes that very clear: "Having predestinated us unto the adoption of children by Jesus Christ to himself, according to the good pleasure of his will, To the praise of the glory of his grace, wherein he hath made us accepted in the beloved."

Once a man believes on the Lord Jesus Christ, he is then predestinated to be conformed to the image of Jesus Christ. And that's done by the good pleasure of His will. In fact, please turn to John chapter 1. Look at verse 11 please: "He came unto his own [the Jews], and his own received him not. But as many as received him [Gentiles], to them gave he power to become the sons of God, *even* to them that believe on his name: Which were born, not of blood, nor of the will of the flesh, nor of the will of man, but of God."

The same sort of language is found very clearly there in reference to the new birth. The source of the new birth is from God, not man.

You cannot get saved by going to church or being a *good* boy or a *good* girl. You are saved by receiving the <u>free gift</u> which God has given to the world before the foundation of the world. "The just shall live by faith" (Romans 1:17b).

Please turn back to Ephesians 1.

VERSES 7-12: "In whom we have redemption through his blood, the forgiveness of sins, according to the riches of his grace; Wherein he hath abounded toward us in all wisdom and prudence; Having made known unto us the mystery of his will, according to his good pleasure which he hath purposed in himself: That in the dispensation of the fulness of times he might gather together in one all things in Christ, both which are in heaven, and which are on earth; *even* **in him: In whom also we have obtained an inheritance, being predestinated according to the purpose of him who worketh all things after the counsel of his own will: That we should be to the praise of his glory, who first trusted in Christ."**

And verse 12 explains even further how you got saved. You are saved by trusting in Christ. You are saved by believing on the Lord Jesus Christ and believing in His death, burial and resurrection. That's what put you into Christ as a living organism: your faith, your trust and your belief. John chapter 1: to as many as received him, to them gave he the right or the power or the authority to become the sons of God.

And although Paul started this epistle dealing with salvation from the standpoint of the Lord's sovereignty from eternity past, he gets to verse 12 where he makes it so very clear: "That we should be to the praise of his glory, who first trusted in Christ." In time, of course. Not before the foundation of the world. Nobody was in Christ before the foundation of the world. That's a Mormon belief!

Before the foundation of the world, God was the only person that existed. Not even the angels existed. Just God! But, yes, in the mind of the Lord, before the foundation of the world,

He knew those that were going to believe on Him and those that would not.

Verse 7: We have received redemption through His blood, His precious divine blood. Even the forgiveness of sins past, present and future! Why? According to the riches of His grace. There's that word again: grace. God's unmerited favour.

And verse 9: "Having made known unto us [the saints and faithful from verse 1] the mystery of his will". The New Testament plan of salvation – the church *per se* – was hidden back in the days of the Old Testament.

But this concept, this mystery, was revealed to the apostle Paul "according to his good pleasure (in reference to God) which he hath purposed in himself: That in the dispensation of the fulness of times he might gather together in one all things in Christ, both which are in heaven [the saved], and which are on earth [the living]; *even* in him: In whom also we have obtained an inheritance, being predestinated according to the purpose of him who worketh all things after the counsel of his own will."

The Lord God of the Bible is totally sovereign, that we should be to the praise of His glory who first trusted in Christ.

You have to believe on Him, you have to receive Him to be saved. And only you can do that. Yes, God made it possible for all of the world to be saved through His unlimited atonement, but each and every one of us has to personally appropriate the atonement in order to be saved: "The just shall live by faith".

But, let's move on.

VERSES 13-14: "In whom ye also *trusted*, after that ye heard the word of truth, the gospel of your salvation: in whom also after that ye believed, ye were sealed with that holy Spirit of promise, Which is the earnest of our inheritance

until the redemption of the purchased possession, unto the praise of his glory."

"Faith *cometh* by hearing and hearing by the word of God" (Romans 10:17). And that word, again, "trusted" is synonymous with faith which is synonymous with the just living by faith. We don't live by sight, we live by faith. And the Lord Jesus Christ told Thomas how blessed he had been to have seen the risen Christ, but blessed are those that have not seen the risen Christ and yet have still been saved by believing. What a great gift awaits such people!

Verse 13: "in whom also after that ye believed". No works involved! You were sealed with that Holy Spirit of promise. Sealed (chapter 4, verse 30) until the day of redemption, which comes after your death, which specifically would be in reference to you arriving at the Judgment Seat of Christ. And the Holy Spirit (being the Holy Ghost, of course) seals you and He and He alone keeps you sealed until the judgment seat of Christ. If you're born again, you are forever born again and you are kept forever saved. Through no works of your own! It's all totally down to the grace and mercy and love of the Lord Jesus Christ.

And also two words from 11 and 14: "inheritance". It could be in reference to salvation *per se*, but more likely to be in reference to the millennial kingdom, found in 1 Corinthians chapter 6. More on that later.

VERSES 15-23: "Wherefore I also, after I heard of your faith in the Lord Jesus, and love unto all the saints, Cease not to give thanks for you, making mention of you in my prayers; That the God of our Lord Jesus Christ, the Father of glory, may give unto you the spirit of wisdom and revelation in the knowledge of him: The eyes of your understanding

being enlightened; that ye may know what is the hope of his calling, and what the riches of the glory of his inheritance in the saints, And what *is* the exceeding greatness of his power to us-ward who believe, according to the working of his mighty power, Which he wrought in Christ, when he raised him from the dead, and set *him* at his own right hand in the heavenly *places*, Far above all principality, and power, and might, and dominion, and every name that is named, not only in this world, but also in that which is to come: And hath put all *things* under his feet, and gave him *to be* the head over all *things* to the church, Which is his body, the fulness of him that filleth all in all."

Several verses there, and several colons and commas and semi-colons. And this is very much a style of the apostle Paul. Once he got on a roll, away he goes! So many verses covered here and so much doctrine and theology, which is essential to the saints of God if you ever wish to grow in grace.

And all born-again Bible-believing Christians are automatically saints made by the Lord God of the Bible upon receiving the new birth. No church can make you a saint. Only the Lord God of the Bible can do so the moment you believe and receive and trusted (there's that word again!) in Christ Jesus to save you from all of your past, present and future sins.

But let's look at these verses in a little more detail if we may. In verse 16, Paul continues to pray without ceasing for the church in Ephesus. If he did so, we should be praying for one another as well: that the God of our Lord Jesus Christ, the Father of glory may give unto you the spirit of wisdom and revelation in the knowledge of Him.

That comes, of course, first of all through the new birth and secondly through the word of God. Read it, study it, and apply it as best as you can, that "the eyes of your understanding being enlightened, that ye may know what is the hope of his calling, and what the riches of the glory of his inheritance in the saints". Not your physical eyes, of course, even though your physical eyes read the written word of God, but your spiritual eyes. "The just shall live by faith." "For we walk by faith, not by sight."

To know the will of God, you have to know the word of God. And that's why it's imperative to read it each and every day without fail. Not only to stop yourself from backsliding, but to know what the hope of His calling is for your life.

And he goes on to say: "And what *is* the exceeding greatness of his power to us-ward who believe [who trusted, who received], according to the working of his mighty power." You can't miss it. It's faith in Christ alone. No works involved whatsoever.

Verse 20: "Which he [God] wrought in Christ, when he raised him from the dead." God the Father resurrected the Lord Jesus Christ (Galatians chapter 1), the Holy Spirit resurrected the Lord Jesus Christ (Romans chapter 8) and God the Son resurrected Himself from the dead (John chapter 2).

"And set *him* [Jesus] at his own right hand in the heavenly places," which would be the third heaven, of course. If you fly in a plane anywhere you are technically flying through space, which would be the first heaven. When you see astronauts flying to the space station, that would be the second heaven. But God Himself lives in a third heaven, far north.

And he goes on to say in verse 21: "Far above all principality [meaning angels, demons, spiritual beings], and power, and might, and dominion and every name that is named, not only in this world [kings, presidents, and prime ministers] but also in that which is to come [the second coming of Christ, the millennial reign to be precise]: and hath put all *things* [without exception] under his feet [meaning He has conquered death], and gave him [Jesus] *to be* the head over all *things* to the church."

The Pope is not the head of the church, nor is the Archbishop of Canterbury, or an apostle or a pastor or an evangelist. Jesus Christ is the Head of the Church, "which is his body, the fulness of Him that filleth all in all." He's omnipresent. He's omnipotent, and He's omniscient. To fill "all in all" means He's everywhere at the same time, proving He is deity.

So, a quick recap on Ephesians chapter 1.

Paul was made an apostle of Jesus Christ by Jesus Christ Himself. Totally independent of the early church. And he's writing to the saints which are in Ephesus and to the faithful in Christ Jesus, in reference to a person's eternal security and in reference to a person's standing in the Lord Jesus Christ. The moment you believed and received and trusted in the death, burial and resurrection of the Lord Jesus Christ, you were made a saint by the Lord God of the Bible. Incredible!

No church can make a man a saint. Only God Himself can make a man or woman a saint, but that is conditional on you believing in Jesus Christ to save you from all of your past, present and future sins. And on top of that, he goes on to tell us in verse 3 how God has already blessed us with all spiritual blessings in heavenly places in Christ. All without exception! And heavenly places (one more time) will be the third heaven, which means you are already in Heaven (spiritually speaking, of course) if you have been born again. And he goes on to say in verse 4:

"According as he [God] hath chosen us [those of us which have appropriated the atonement in time] in him [Jesus] before the foundation of the world, that we [the Church, those of us which have appropriated the atonement] should be holy and without blame before him in love" which comes from Christ's imputed righteousness.

Nothing we do can make us right with God. Our righteousness is as filthy rags in the presence of God. But Christ's righteousness is sinless. When God looks at a saved person, He sees Jesus Christ, not the saved person.

And Paul moves on: "Having predestinated us [those of us which have appropriated the atonement in time] unto the adoption of children by Jesus Christ himself, according to the good pleasure of his will."

This can only happen because God has allowed it to happen. He's made it possible to happen because of His good pleasure. "To the praise of the glory of his grace [verse 6] wherein he hath made us accepted in the beloved." Past tense!

In the Old Testament, to approach God you would have to go either through the temple or the priest or a sacrifice, but now you can come to God directly through the Lord Jesus Christ and through His precious divine blood, He has granted those that have appropriated the atonement the total forgiveness of sins according to the riches of His grace. "Faith alone, grace alone, in Christ alone." *Sola fide*, of course!

Verses 10 and 11: "That in the dispensation of the fulness of times he might gather together in one all things in Christ, both which are in heaven, and which are on earth; *even* in him." That will, no doubt, occur at the end of the Judgment Seat of Christ when He comes back to rule and reign for a thousand years in Jerusalem.

But look at verse 11, please: "In whom also we have obtained an inheritance [not just salvation, but the right to rule and reign with Him, which is still conditioned on how you live after you are saved, and I'll get to that later] being predestinated according to the purpose of him who worketh all things after the counsel of his own will." He's made it possible for those of us which are born again to go into the Millennial Kingdom. He's drawn all men unto Himself (John 6, John 12).

He's granted repentance to the Jews (Acts 5) and to the Gentiles (Acts 11). God was in Christ reconciling the world (not just the elect) unto Himself (2 Corinthians chapter 5), but now He calls all men (without exception) everywhere to repent (Acts 17) and be reconciled to God (2 Corinthians chapter 5), and He's done so due to the counsel of His own will.

He's all powerful, He's omnipresent, He's omnipotent and He's omniscient. But at the same time, your salvation is dependent on trusting in Christ (verse 12). The verses before this point back to the sovereignty of the Lord from eternity past, but verse 12 deals explicitly as to how you got saved. By believing, by receiving, by trusting in Christ when you first heard the gospel of your salvation, "in whom also after that ye believed, ye were sealed with that holy Spirit of promise."

You trusted, you received, you believed. Faith in Christ alone once you heard the gospel of your salvation. And after that, you were sealed by the Holy Spirit of promise. You are in the Beloved. You belong to Him, and He belongs to you. And outside of the triune God, if you are born again, if you have trusted in Him (verse 12), you are the most important person outside of the Trinity as far as God Himself is concerned.

And verses 20 down to 23 speaks explicitly about Jesus Christ being raised up into the heavenly places. And according to Romans chapter 6, if you have believed on Jesus Christ, you were buried with Him and you have been resurrected with Him. You were even baptised into Him the moment you believed on Him (1 Corinthians 12, Ephesians chapter 4).

So, the keywords - as far as I am concerned, from Ephesians chapter 1 - will be provision and appropriation. God has provided an atonement for everyone, but you have to personally appropriate it in order to be saved. So, as far as I'm concerned, verse 12 explains verses 3, 4, 5 and 6.

So, what started with you being predestinated unto the adoption of children by Jesus Christ Himself was explained in verse 12. First of all, you trusted in Christ, and then you were predestinated to be adopted to become a child, to become an heir, to become a friend of Jesus Christ. But that was only possible because of God's good pleasure: "To the praise of the glory of his grace [verse 6] wherein, he hath made us accepted in the beloved."

Salvation, one more time, is all of God. The source of the new birth - John chapter 1 - is of God. You couldn't get saved yourself. Salvation came from God. God has granted repentance to the Jew (Acts 5), to the Gentile (Acts 11) and He's drawn all men unto Himself (John chapter 12). But now He calls all men everywhere to repent (Acts 17) and be reconciled to Himself (2 Corinthians chapter 5). What a merciful God we serve and what a loving Saviour He truly is!

In verse 22, He is the Head over all things to the Church. He is the Rock, He is the foundation, He is everything. Give God the glory!

CHAPTER 2

VERSES 1-3: "And you *hath he quickened*, who were dead in trespasses and sins; Wherein in time past ye walked according to the course of this world, according to the prince of the power of the air, the spirit that now worketh in the children of disobedience: Among whom also we all had our conversation in times past in the lusts of our flesh, fulfilling the desires of the flesh and of the mind; and were by nature the children of wrath, even as others."

Paul says in verse 3 how we all had our conversation (conduct, character) in times past in the lusts of our flesh. He even includes himself in this indictment, fulfilling the desires of the flesh. You lived like the devil before you were saved. You were your own god before you are saved. But God had to crush you, He had to break you, He had to mould you, in order to bring you unto Himself.

Most of us were a wreck before we got saved. And by our minds, by our natures, we were enemies of God, "children of wrath, even as others". We were filthy, we were despicable, we were wicked, and we deserved to go to Hell. But due to His mercy, He's reconciled the world unto Himself.

If God was to give us justice, we would all go to Hell. But He's given us grace, His unmerited favour.

And the prince of the power of the air, from verse 2, would be Satan, of course. We were children of Satan before we became children of the light. In verse 1, He has quickened us who were dead in trespasses and sins.

To be dead in the sense of being the opposite to being alive. To be dead in trespasses and sins does not mean (before you are born again) you did not know the difference between right and wrong, because you did. It simply means you had yet to be regenerated. And Calvinists claim this verse teaches that you are totally depraved, totally incapable of believing on the Lord Jesus Christ unless Jesus Christ did something for you. But that's not what this text teaches.

If you go to Luke chapter 15, the prodigal son was dead. But when he came to himself, he ran back to his father and was reconciled to his father. So, yes, you were quickened. Yes, you were dead in your trespasses and sins pre the new birth which simply means you were yet to be regenerated. You are an enemy of God by your nature, by your mind, by your entire being.

And yes, you deserved to go to Hell, like I say. You deserved to receive the justice of God, but through His grace, He saved you. He did not condemn you, and He did so by quickening you, which means He has spiritually resurrected you already, your spirit being with the Lord in the heavenly places right now, if you are saved.

And I'll say this also before we move on to verse 4. Your flesh, from verse 3, has never been redeemed and will never be redeemed. If you're born again, your flesh is your old man and your flesh will battle with the new man each and every day. In Philippians chapter 3, Paul made it very clear that he had not yet received - he had not yet reached - the level of perfection.

In Romans chapter 7, he made it very clear how he continued to battle the old flesh each and every day of his life. Paul stumbled post his salvation. He was told not to go up to Jerusalem, and he went up nevertheless.

Peter was told in Acts 10 to go to the house of Cornelius, and he argued with the Lord. Peter wilfully committed sin and Paul had to publicly rebuke him in Galatians chapter 2, indicating that he too was battling the flesh.

So, your flesh is your number one enemy. Never mind the devil, never mind heresy, never mind heretics! Your flesh, if you are born again, is your number one enemy, and you were told to put your flesh to death. You were told to mortify your flesh, and you were told to present your flesh (your body) as a living sacrifice unto God (Romans chapter 12) each and every day. "Be ye holy; for I am holy" saith the Lord (I Peter 1:16).

And those that refuse to deal with the flesh and live in perpetual rebellion to the Lord God risk losing their millennial inheritance when they die.

But take a look, please, at verses 4-7: **"But God, who is rich in mercy, for his great love wherewith he loved us, Even when we were dead in sins, hath quickened us together with Christ, (by grace ye are saved;) And hath raised *us* up together, and made us sit together in heavenly *places* in Christ Jesus: That in the ages to come he might shew the exceeding riches of his grace in *his* kindness toward us through Christ Jesus."**

Verse 5: "quickened us together with Christ" even when we were dead in sins. How and why? By grace, God's unmerited favour. And once He did that, He made us sit together with Christ in the heavenly places. Your spirit has been regenerated and your spirit is in Heaven with the Lord today. Spiritually speaking, of course.

"That in the ages to come (verse 7) he might shew the exceeding riches of his grace in *his* kindness toward us through Christ Jesus." Everything in the universe was made by Christ

Jesus and given to Christ Jesus as a gift from God the Father. The Church has been given to Christ Jesus as a gift from the Father. And Christ Jesus gives the Church back to God the Father as a gift.

But verses 1, 5 and 6 speaking about being quickened (being made alive in Christ Jesus and made to sit together in heavenly places in Christ Jesus) is conditioned on trusting on Christ (chapter 1, verse 12).

You were not in Christ until you believed, received and trusted Christ Jesus to save you. Predestination is only relevant when you believed, received and trusted in Christ Jesus.

Until you believed on Him, you were outside of the commonwealth of Israel. You were an enemy of God through your mind, through wicked works. You were a child of the devil, but God has made it possible to reconcile the world unto Himself. How? Through the death, burial and resurrection of the Lord Jesus Christ.

VERSES 8-9: "For by grace are ye saved through faith; and that not of yourselves: *it is* the gift of God: Not of works, lest any man should boast."

Through God's grace, salvation is a free gift totally dependent on the grace of God. And your faith in the grace of God, being Jesus Christ, allows you to be saved. "*It is* the gift of God: Not of works, lest any man should boast."

Going to church will not save you, speaking in tongues will not save you, being circumcised will not save you. Being confirmed, receiving communion, being a Eucharistic minister, a deacon, a pastor, a priest, a vicar, an evangelist will not save you nor is it proof of being saved.

It is the gift of God: "Not of works, lest any man should boast." And this piece of Scripture is quite possibly the clearest in all of Paul's epistles when it comes to salvation being a free gift.

Just believe on Him. Receive Him as a child would, and then you will be happily saved until the Judgment Seat of Christ.

Your salvation cannot be lost but your millennial inheritance - if you're not careful, if you live after the flesh after you have been saved and don't repent - might be lost. But more on that later.

VERSE 10: "For we are his workmanship, created in Christ Jesus unto good works, which God hath before ordained that we should walk in them."

Before we believed on the Lord Jesus Christ, He ordained that we should walk in good works. You can never do enough good works after you are born again. But please remember this: that your good works will not save you and your good works will not earn you favour or merit with God if you are not truly born again.

You do good works because you are saved, not in order to be saved or in order to stay saved. But your good works may be a deciding factor when it comes to the Judgment Seat of Christ, as to which rewards the Lord Jesus Christ gives you.

So, for salvation, it makes no difference whatsoever, but for your rewards at the Judgment Seat of Christ and subsequent entrance into the millennial kingdom of God, your good works could make all the difference. So, be busy for the Lord and whatever you do for the Lord, make sure you do it through the Spirit, not the flesh.

But let's look at verses 11-13, please: **"Wherefore remember, that ye *being* in time past Gentiles in the flesh, who are called Uncircumcision by that which is called the**

Circumcision in the flesh made by hands; That at that time ye were without Christ, being aliens from the commonwealth of Israel, and strangers from the covenants of promise, having no hope, and without God in the world: But now in Christ Jesus ye who sometimes were far off are made nigh by the blood of Christ."

Remarkable! Before you were saved, you were outside of the kingdom of God. You were an enemy of God. You had no hope. You were almost in spiritual blindness. But now through the precious blood of Christ, you have been brought near to Him.

VERSES 14-17: "For he is our peace, who hath made both one, and hath broken down the middle wall of partition *between us*; **Having abolished in his flesh the enmity,** *even* **the law of commandments** *contained* **in ordinances; for to make in himself of twain one new man, so making peace; And that he might reconcile both unto God in one body by the cross, having slain the enmity thereby: And came and preached peace to you which were afar off, and to them that were nigh."**

It was always His plan to bring Jew and Gentile together to make for Himself one man. In John 10, He told the Jews how He had sheep that were not yet of His fold, in reference to the Gentiles.

Jesus Christ may have been Jewish. The Bible may be a Jewish book, but the Jewish Messiah is the Messiah for the Jew and the Gentile. If the Jew and Gentile came to Jesus Christ tomorrow, there would almost be worldwide peace. You wouldn't need a police force or an army or a navy or an air force any more. Man wouldn't be sinless *per se*, but sin in general would severely decline.

And if Jew and Muslim would come to Jesus Christ today, there would almost be peace in the Middle East. He's made it possible to reconcile Jew and Gentile unto Himself. Man and woman unto Himself. Boy and girl unto Himself.

But you've got to come to Him. Man has a free will, while God is sovereign at the same time. The two seem to contradict, but they don't. It's simply a paradox.

And verses 11, 12, 13, and 14 and 15 are so remarkable. The Gentiles were called the uncircumcision. They were considered to be unclean by the circumcision, being the Jews. But the circumcision, which the Jews almost rejoiced in, almost boasted in, has now become worthless because through the precious blood of the Lord Jesus Christ, those "which were afar off" have now been brought nigh by His precious blood. And we have peace (verse 14) because He has "broken down the middle wall of partition *between us*."

According to Galatians chapter 3, if you are born again, you are neither Jewish nor Gentile. You are simply in Christ Jesus.

And he goes on to say in verse 15: "Having abolished in his flesh [His literal body] the enmity, *even* the law of commandments *contained* in ordinances." You are not, therefore, under the law any more. You are under grace. You live in the new covenant, not in the old covenant. And He's made in Himself one new man. Jew and Gentile are no more. If you're born again, you are born again and you should simply offer yourself as a born-again Bible-believing Christian.

And also from verse 15, "Having abolished in his flesh the enmity." The consequences of our sins but even more than that, the law of commandments. The law points you to the Saviour. The law makes it very clear that you are a lawbreaker in need of punishment. You cannot keep the law. The Old Testament prophets could not keep the law. The apostles could not keep the law. Only Jesus Christ kept the law perfectly. Why? Because He's God, pure and simple. You can't keep the law, but He did it for you and, therefore, when He died on the cross, He fulfilled the law for you. All of your sins were put on His account, and after three days God resurrected Him from the dead.

So, when God sees you, if you have been born again, He sees His Son, the perfect sinless Saviour, "the Lamb of God, which taketh away the sins of the world" (John 1:29).

In verse 17, one more time: "And came and preached peace to you which were afar off [outside of the Kingdom of God, totally in darkness, alienated from God through your wicked works], and to them that were nigh."

Even His own people needed to be reconciled to Him because they had drifted from Him through their tradition, through their sinfulness, through their wickedness.

And the word of God tells us how He has come "to seek and to save that which was lost" (Luke 19:10, Matthew 18:11). Remarkable! We deserve justice, but He gives us grace. But you personally have to believe on Him. You have to receive Him and you have to trust in Him to receive His grace, not His justice.

VERSE 18: "For through him we both have access by one Spirit unto the Father."

Unprecedented! Pre the new birth, pre the new covenant, you couldn't come to God unless you went via the temple or the priest or through your sacrifice. But now, through the Holy Spirit we have access unto the Father through Him. "I am the way, the truth, and the life" (John 14:6).

There is only one Saviour, only "one Mediator between God and men, the man Christ Jesus" (1 Timothy 2:5). No one else can do it for you. You've got to come to God through His only begotten Son, the Lord Jesus Christ.

VERSES 19-21: "Now therefore ye are no more strangers and foreigners, but fellowcitizens with the saints, and of the household of God; And are built upon the foundation of the apostles and prophets, Jesus Christ himself being the chief corner *stone*; In whom all the building fitly framed together groweth unto an holy temple in the Lord: In whom ye also are builded together for an habitation of God through the Spirit."

The Church is built on the apostles and prophets, with Jesus Christ Himself being the chief cornerstone, the Rock. Not Simon Peter, but Jesus Christ. And that's past tense also. There are no apostles or prophets today. An apostle was an eyewitness of the Lord Jesus Christ, and a prophet - like Ezekiel, Jeremiah and Isaiah - foresaw and foretold the future.

We now live by faith. "The just shall live by faith." And so our foundation is past tense, "built", past tense, on the apostles, prophets and Jesus Christ.

So, to recap Ephesians chapter 2, if we may, God has quickened us while we were dead in our trespasses and sins because we trusted in Him (chapter 1, verse 12), and then He resurrected us. He raised us in a spiritual sense (verses 5 and 6 from chapter 2) and has made us sit together in heavenly places in Christ Jesus. We are in Christ Jesus and we are also in God the Father and God the Holy Ghost.

And just in case you missed it, from verse 9, you weren't saved by your works, but by grace (verse 8) through faith in Jesus

Christ "and that not of yourselves: *it is* the gift of God". The new birth comes from God, not man. Man cannot save himself and nor can he keep himself saved by his works.

The Son of Man has drawn all men unto Himself, and He came to seek and to save that which was lost. Chapter 1, verse 12, one last time: "That we should be to the praise of his glory [it's all His glory, it's all about Him] who first trusted in Christ."

Chapter 2, verse 8: "For by grace are ye saved through faith [no works involved whatsoever]; and that not of yourselves."

"I've believed on the Lord Jesus Christ, I'm now a Bible-believing Christian, aren't I wonderful person?" No, you're not. You believed on Him because He granted you repentance (Acts 5, Acts 11). He drew you unto Himself and He reconciled the world unto Himself (2 Corinthians chapter 5), but now is the day of salvation. Today is the day of salvation. You need to believe on Him in order to be saved.

But he goes on to say in chapter 2, verse 10, how we have been "created in Christ Jesus unto good works which God hath before ordained that we should walk in them."

Before we believed on Him, He ordained it that each and everyone of us would have works which would follow our salvation. And that's what James chapter 2 is all about. "Faith without works is dead" (chapter 2, verse 20) and works without faith is dead as well. If you're saved you will produce works and your works will justify that you are saved. But don't trust in your works in order to save you or to keep you saved. And make sure your works are found in Scripture. Make sure your works are as a result of the Spirit, not of the flesh.

In verse 11, circumcision for the Jew in the Old Testament was done physically. But circumcision in the New Testament is done spiritually, and it's in the heart, not elsewhere.

Pre the New Covenant, Gentiles were without Christ. They were aliens from the commonwealth of Israel. They may just as well have been living on another planet. And they were strangers from the covenants of promise because the covenants were given to the children of Israel, not the Gentiles.

The Ten Commandments were given to the children of Israel, not the Gentiles. They had no hope, and they were without God in the world, orphans if you will.

But now, through the new birth (verse 13) in Christ Jesus "ye [plural, those of you which have appropriated the atonement] who sometimes were afar off are made nigh by the [precious] blood of Christ. That "he [Jesus, verse 14] is our peace." He's our bridge between heaven and earth, between God and men. And He "hath made both one [Jew and Gentile], and hath broken down the middle wall of partition *between us.*"

The Jews had a physical temple with physical walls, which to some extent was to keep the Gentiles out. But now, He's knocked down not just the physical walls, but the spiritual walls as well, "Having abolished in his flesh [verse 15] the enmity [which would be sin], *even* the law of commandments *contained* in ordinances; for to make in himself of twain one new man, so making peace; And that he might reconcile both unto God in one body by the cross, having slain the enmity thereby". A physical cross, not a stake as the Jehovah's Witnesses would have you believe. And He did literally hang on a cross, unlike what the Muslims would have you believe.

In verse 17, He "came and preached peace to you which were afar off [Gentiles], and to them that were nigh [the people of Israel].

In verse 18, "For through him [Jesus] we both have access by one Spirit unto the Father [Jew and Gentile]. Come to Him if you need Him! Come to His throne of grace in a moment of crisis! Call Him "Abba, Father" and He will hear you, He will receive you, and He will grant you peace which is totally supernatural and not of this world.

In verse 19, Paul looks beyond your justification and sanctification, and he says, "Now therefore, ye are no more strangers and foreigners, but fellowcitizens with the saints, and of the household of God," which is spiritual now but it will be physical during the millennial kingdom of God. And this goes back to the earlier verses from chapter 1, verses 3, 4 and 5, in reference to being predestinated to be conformed to the image of Christ Jesus, to be made a child of God through adoption.

"And are built [past tense] upon the foundation of the apostles and prophets, Jesus Christ himself being the chief corner *stone* [verse 20]; In whom all the building fitly framed together groweth [as more believe on Him] unto an holy temple in the Lord [not a physical temple, but a spiritual temple]: In whom ye also a builded together for an habitation of God through the Spirit."

For here and now, we live in a spiritual kingdom (those of us which are born again), but when Jesus Christ comes back to rule and reign in Jerusalem for a thousand years, we will be with Him in a physical kingdom. And we will be priests and kings to Him, ruling and reining with Him for a thousand years.

So, for those of us which are born again and living today in the Church age, we are in a spiritual kingdom of God. But at the end of the Great Tribulation, when the Lord Jesus Christ comes back to earth from Heaven, we come back with Him to rule and reign for one thousand literal years in the physical kingdom of God.

Your salvation is solely dependent on what He did for you by dying on the cross. But to fully and unconditionally rule and reign with Him for a thousand years is dependent on what you do for Him after you've been born again by believing on Him who died on the cross for your sins.

And the reason why we come back with Him at the end of the Great Tribulation is because we were raptured with Him before the Great Tribulation. But more on that as we go through the Book of the Ephesians.

CHAPTER 3

VERSES 1-7: "For this cause I Paul, the prisoner of Jesus Christ for you Gentiles, If ye have heard of the dispensation of the grace of God which is given me to you-ward: How that by revelation he made known unto me the mystery; (as I wrote afore in few words, Whereby, when ye read, ye may understand my knowledge in the mystery of Christ) Which in other ages was not made known unto the sons of men, as it is now revealed unto his holy apostles and prophets by the Spirit; That the Gentiles should be fellowheirs, and of the same body, and partakers of his promise in Christ by the gospel: Whereof I was made a minister, according to the gift of the grace of God given unto me by the effectual working of his power."

He calls himself a prisoner in verse 1. Not holy father, not your Eminence, not even pastor or reverend or deacon. Elsewhere he would call himself "Paul, the aged," but here he calls himself a prisoner. Paul was as about as free as one could possibly be, and yet he considered himself to be a prisoner, a servant, a slave, of the Lord Jesus Christ. He was in the service of the Lord, he was in the army of the Lord, and he loved it.

And he goes on to say how his mystery gospel was veiled back in the Old Testament, but it was revealed to the apostle Paul in Acts chapter 9.

No church ordained him. No church called for him to serve alongside them. It was all done by the Lord God of the Bible. And he says the apostles were holy in verse 5, not in and of themselves, of course. They too needed to be born again. But the

Bible tells us how "holy men of God spake as they *were moved* by the Holy Ghost" (2 Peter 1:21), which means that the Bible is inspired through their writings, not through the writers *per se*.

In verse 7, he calls himself a minister, which if you cross-reference it back to verse 1, being a prisoner, simply means a servant. Paul the apostle did not wear a dog collar or a mitre. He was not called father, reverend, doctor, professor or your grace. He was simply called a prisoner and a minister of the Lord Jesus Christ, called by Jesus Christ (not by any church) to do what he was going to do for the Lord God of the Holy Bible.

And these verses are a reaffirmation of the last chapter, how the gospel of the grace of God was hidden to the Jews back in the Old Testament, although the writers of the Old Testament did allude to it in many places.

But, nevertheless, it was revealed fully and clearly to the apostle Paul in the New Testament, and here he is reaffirming what he's already told us from the last chapter how the Gentiles are going to be grafted into the Jewish root, which you find very clearly in Romans 11, and they too will become the people of God.

Look at verses 8-12, please: **"Unto me, who am less than the least of all saints, is this grace given, that I should preach among the Gentiles the unsearchable riches of Christ; And to make all *men* see what *is* the fellowship of the mystery, which from the beginning of the world hath been hid in God, who created all things by Jesus Christ: To the intent that now unto the principalities and powers in heavenly *places* might be known by the church the manifold wisdom of God, According to the eternal purpose which he purposed in**

Christ Jesus our Lord: In whom we have boldness and access with confidence by the faith of him."

In verse 8, he calls himself 'less than all the saints' and yet in reality he was the greatest of all of the saints. He wrote most of the New Testament. He was sent to the Gentiles. Peter was sent to the Jews. He suffered the most and yet loved the most. Especially the Jews who hated him with a perfect hatred.

The Lord Jesus Christ lived on the earth for three and a half years and he chose 12 men out of over 82 men. None of those men were chosen to do what Paul did, and yet Paul as a prisoner in verse 1 and a minister in verse 7 said he was the least of all the saints. That is humility!

As I have said previously: you won't find people like Paul calling himself holy father, or reverend or his eminence. In fact, in the Epistle to the Corinthians he almost called himself scum, and elsewhere in the New Testament, he said he was a murderer who persecuted the Church of God.

But over time he healed from some of that pain and was able to rejoice through his sufferings. He was a writer, he was a scholar. And yet through his poor eyesight, he ended up having to rely on his scribes. He would dictate his epistles to them; they would write his epistles for him and read his epistles back to him. And for me, I believe that was his thorn in the flesh.

For a scholar, for a writer, to no longer be able to read and write and have to rely on others to do it for you is probably one of the hardest things to live with. And yet Jesus told him, in Acts 9, how he (Paul) would suffer many things for the sake of the Lord Jesus Christ.

In verse 12, he says, "we have boldness and access with confidence by the faith of him."

Most pagan religions around the world, even to this present time, fear their deities and they sacrifice to their deities. Most of India is still very much in darkness and the River Ganges is a filthy lake where animals wash in and urinate in, and yet superstitious, ignorant Indians will go along and bathe in that water, expecting to receive a blessing from one of their many deities. They have no boldness or confidence when they approach their deity.

But here, Paul says we which have been born again "have boldness and access with confidence by the faith of him." Faith alone to be saved and faith alone to receive confidence and boldness when we approach His throne of grace. Remarkable!

VERSE 13: "Wherefore I desire that ye faint not at my tribulations for you, which is your glory."

Paul's saying, 'Don't worry about me. Yes, my life is hard. Yes, I've been stoned and shipwrecked and left for dead on many occasions. And yes, I live hand to mouth for the most part for your sakes. But "I can do all things through Christ which strengtheneth me" (Philippians 4:13).

Paul was such a remarkable man and I believe what he forgot we will never know when it comes to how to truly live for the Lord God of the Bible.

VERSES 14-19: "For this cause I bow my knees unto the Father of our Lord Jesus Christ, Of whom the whole family in heaven and earth is named, That he would grant you, according to the riches of his glory, to be strengthened with might by his Spirit in the inner man; That Christ may dwell in your hearts by faith; that ye, being rooted and grounded in love, May be able to comprehend with all saints what *is* the breadth, and length, and depth, and height; And to know

the love of Christ, which passeth knowledge, that ye might be filled with all the fulness of God."

In verse 14, Paul bows his knees unto the Father of our Lord Jesus Christ, of whom the whole family in heaven and earth is named, those that are saved - and Paul goes on to tell us in 2 Corinthians that to be absent from the body meant to be present with the Lord. A saved person that died post-Pentecost went straight to be with the Lord Jesus Christ. Pre-Pentecost, a saved believer went into the ground, Abraham's bosom. But post-Pentecost, a saved party that dies believing in the Lord Jesus Christ goes straight to be with Him. Their bodies sleep, but their souls go straight to be with the Lord Jesus Christ.

And He wants you to grow. He wants you to be strengthened in the inner man (from verse 16), which goes back to what I said last time from Romans 12: how we (all of us) are to present our bodies every day as a living sacrifice to God. Why? So, we grow in grace, we don't commit the sins of the flesh, but we grow in grace, to be rooted and grounded in love (verse 17), that Christ may dwell in our hearts by faith.

In verse 18, he pretty much reaffirms how all the saints are going to be able to comprehend "what *is* the breadth, and length, and depth, and height" in reference to the "love of Christ [found in verse 19], which passeth knowledge, that ye [all of you] might be filled with all the fulness of God."

As I said earlier, outside of the triune God, if you are born again, you are the most important person in the universe to God. And He wants to fill all of his children with the fulness of Himself. You don't become deity, of course, but through the adoption, you become the sons and daughters of the living God.

Look at verses 20-21, please: **"Now unto him that is able to do exceeding abundantly above all that we ask or think, according to the power that worketh in us, Unto him *be* glory in the church by Christ Jesus throughout all ages, world without end. Amen."**

He can do everything abundantly, even above what we ask or even think because He is all-powerful and, therefore, to Him all the glory is due and worthy to be given to Him.

"World without end," in reference to the saint living forever when time is no longer in existence. "Amen," meaning "so let it be."

So, to recap on Ephesians chapter 3, Paul reaffirms his credentials as an apostle. He reaffirms what he told us from the last chapter: how it was always going to be the Lord's will to have just one people (Jew and Gentile) worshipping Him in truth and in spirit via the new birth. A new creation.

And through humility, Paul was able to grow in grace and the same is true of us today. Never give up on prayer, because God "is able to do exceeding abundantly above all that we ask or think, according to the power that worketh in us". But it's got to be according to His will and we have to be in the Spirit, not in the flesh, when we pray to the Father and always in the name of the Lord Jesus Christ.

And the last word from chapter 3 (that being "Amen") almost suggests that Paul has finished Ephesians, but not quite. We have three more chapters to go, and the meat of Scripture gets better. The content gets deeper, and the truth of Christ gets richer.

CHAPTER 4

VERSES 1-3: "I therefore, the prisoner of the Lord, beseech you that ye walk worthy of the vocation wherewith ye are called, With all lowliness and meekness, with longsuffering, forbearing one another in love; Endeavouring to keep the unity of the Spirit in the bond of peace."

This is the second time that Paul has called himself a prisoner. We saw it very clearly from chapter 3, verse 1. And like I said last time, Paul didn't call himself holy father, reverend, your eminence or your grace. Simply a prisoner in reference to his service to the Lord.

And this word 'vocation' (also found in chapter 4, verse 1) is in reference to all born-again Bible-believing Christians. Sometimes people say, "my vocation is to be a priest or a vicar or a pastor." But Paul is not speaking to elders or leaders in the church. He is speaking to all Bible-believing Christians in Ephesus, called "saints," called "faithful" (from chapter 1, verse 1).

And he goes on to say in verse 2 and 3, "With all lowliness and meekness, with longsuffering, forbearing one another in love; Endeavouring to keep the unity of the Spirit in the bond of peace."

If you love the brethren, you are doing very well. If you do not love the brethren, the word of God tells us from 1 John chapter 3 that something is wrong with you. You have fallen from grace. You have lost your fellowship with the Lord.

In fact, the word of God tell us that if you hate your brother (1 John chapter 3), you are a murderer, and no murderer has everlasting life abiding in them. So if you hate someone who is born again, something is severely wrong with you. You're either not saved, or more likely you have fallen from grace. Confess your sins to Him. And 1 John chapter 1 says He [Jesus] is faithful and just to forgive you of all of your sins and to cleanse you of your unrighteousness.

But look at verse 4-6 please: **"*There is* one body, and one Spirit, even as ye are called in one hope of your calling; One Lord, one faith, one baptism, One God and Father of all, who *is* above all, and through all, and in you all."**

Chapter 1, verse 1: The faithful and the saints are in Christ Jesus. Chapter 1, verse 3: we have been blessed "with all spiritual blessings in heavenly *places* in Christ."

And here we see it so very clearly in verse 6: how God the Father is in all of you. So, the triune God - if you are born again - lives within you. The Father, the Son and the Holy Ghost.

But go back to verse 4, please. "*There is* one body [in reference to the church], and one Spirit [Holy Ghost], even as ye are called in one hope of your calling; One Lord, one faith, one baptism."

Break it down: the Body of Christ is diverse, yes. And there are many different denominations and many groups within groups of born-again Bible-believing Christians. But if they are in Christ Jesus, they are in His one Body, which demonstrates the diversity of God. Many saints worshipping Him all over the world in different ways in different time zones from different cultures because He has allowed them to worship Him in ways of their own choosing.

But you have to be in Christ Jesus to be in His one Body. "One Lord [the triune God], one faith [Christianity], one baptism [spiritual, not through water baptism], one God and Father of all, who *is* above all [the only one true God], and through all [not a pantheist], and in you all [in reference to those which have appropriated the atonement]."

So, yes, there are many churches but the Lord Jesus Christ told us where two or three meet to worship Him, He is there in the midst of them.

Go back to the Old Testament: to form a synagogue, you needed at least 12 Jewish men. But Jesus says, forget that, where just two or three people meet to worship me and break bread, I am there in the midst of them. And that, of course, would constitute a church, a local fellowship.

But let's move on, verse 7, please: **"But unto every one of us is given grace according to the measure of the gift of Christ.**

In reference to a person's faith. Some people have been called to be missionaries and some people would die overseas for their faith in the Lord Jesus Christ. Others have been called to be street preachers or ministers. Some have been called to be pastors or deacons, and some people have been gifted to be a jack-of-all-trades, meaning they can do a bit of everything.

So while the Lord has called us all the same way to be saved and serve Him, we have not all been equipped with the same gift. Some will do greater things for the Lord, based on what they can do, through the Lord's foreknowledge, of course.

VERSES 8-9: "Wherefore he saith, When he ascended up on high, he led captivity captive, and gave gifts unto men. (Now that he ascended, what is it but that he also descended first into the lower parts of the earth?"

This would be in reference to the Lord's Ascension. Pre-His death, burial and resurrection, all the righteous dead - all those that died believing the one true God - went into the ground and they waited in the ground for the Messiah to go and get them (Luke chapter 16), known as Abraham's bosom. And that place in the ground is referred back in the Old Testament as the Pit, Sheol, Tartarus, Hades, Gehenna. And this location in the ground had two parts: one part was for the righteous dead and the other part was for the unrighteous dead. And the rich man in Hell could see Abraham and Lazarus. And Abraham said to him: you cannot come to us and we cannot go to you, meaning once you die in your sins, there's no second chance for you. And if you died in the Lord, you're kept saved in the Lord.

But this Scripture makes it very clear how Jesus Christ descended first into the lower parts of the earth. Hell, yes, but not into the area of the unrighteous wicked dead. Jesus Christ went into the area of the righteous dead: Abraham, Isaac, Jacob and the beggar. And from there, He preached victory to the unrighteous wicked dead. No more than that.

And no, He was not the first born-again man. Jesus Christ did not need to go to Hell to suffer any more for our sins. When He hung on the cross, one of the last things He said was, "It is finished." And it was. All on the cross, not in the ground! But He's got to go into the ground to release the righteous dead.

But look at verse 10, please: **"He that descended is the same also that ascended up far above all heavens, that he might fill all things.)"**

To be absent from the body is to be present with the Lord. So, take verses 8 down to 10 together (and it's so very clear how the Lord Jesus Christ went into the lower parts of the earth after dying to set captivity captive, those that died believing in the one true God), and the unrighteous dead are still there to the present day, awaiting the Great White Throne Judgment, of course.

VERSES 11-16: "And he gave some, apostles; and some, prophets; and some, evangelists; and some, pastors and teachers; For the perfecting of the saints, for the work of the ministry, for the edifying of the body of Christ: Till we all come in the unity of the faith, and of the knowledge of the Son of God, unto a perfect man, unto the measure of the stature of the fulness of Christ: That we *henceforth* be no more children, tossed to and fro, and carried about with every wind of doctrine, by the sleight of men, and cunning craftiness, whereby they lie in wait to deceive; But speaking the truth in love, may grow up into him in all things, which is the head, *even* Christ: From whom the whole body fitly joined together and compacted by that which every joint supplieth, according to the effectual working in the measure of every part, maketh increase of the body unto the edifying of itself in love."

He gave (past tense) apostles (verse 11), prophets, evangelists, pastors and teachers. This is all past tense. "For the perfecting of the saints." This was all done pre the completion of the New Testament. There are no more apostles or prophets today. Yes, there were some prophets given during the Acts period from law to grace. And some of those prophets could foresee the future, Agabus being one of them.

But once the New Testament was completed, the saint was told from Romans chapter 1, how "the just shall live by faith," not through sight and not based on prophets foretelling the future.

So, as far as I'm concerned for today, yes, there may be some teachers, elders or Bible teachers which have been gifted to teach the flock at a national or international level, but there are certainly no apostles, prophets or evangelists in the sense of being able to do sign gifts, being able to perform miracles that were done primarily to authenticate the ministry of the apostles who wrote the New Testament.

And, of course, the reason to have skilled born-again Bible-believing elders at a national and international level would be to a) edify the church (grow them in grace, of course) and b) to stop them from being tossed to and fro by false doctrine, by false religions, by the sleight of men (verse 14) "and cunning craftiness."

This once again demonstrates a philosophical problem based on false teachings, and this is why it is imperative to read the word of God each and every day. Believe it. Obey it. And if you are able to teach it to others, do so. Because a little leaven leavens the whole lump, and false doctrine can lead to carnality, which ultimately can lead to a Christian ruining their testimony. In the worst-case scenario, arriving at the Judgment Seat of Christ to receive nothing but condemnation from the Lord Jesus Christ. And of course, Paul is going to build on this stern warning.

VERSES 17-19: "This I say therefore, and testify in the Lord, that ye henceforth walk not as other Gentiles walk, in the vanity of their mind, Having the understanding darkened, being alienated from the life of God through the ignorance that is in them, because of the blindness of their heart: Who being past feeling have given themselves over unto lasciviousness, to work all uncleanness with greediness."

And Paul gives this warning to make it very clear that Christians - if they are not careful - can fall back into their old ways. They can resurrect the old man through the "vanity of their mind... being alienated from the life of God through the ignorance that is in them." Ignorance is no excuse of the law, and ignorance of God and the Bible is no excuse either.

Look at verse 19 one more time: "Who being past feeling." They couldn't care less, they "have given themselves over unto lasciviousness [carnality, wickedness] to work all uncleanness with greediness." Man gives himself, first of all, over to sin. And if he stays in that way of life, the Lord God (according to Romans chapter 1) then permanently abandons him. And once that happens, there's no second chance for such a person. And that, of course, is why the road to Hell is wide "and many there be which go in thereat" (Matthew 7:13). But the gate - the entrance, the way to heaven, everlasting life - is narrow and "few there be which find [the way]" (Matthew 7:14), being Jesus Christ, of course.

So, if you're saved, your worst enemy is your flesh, and if you're not saved, your worst enemy is also your flesh.

And it's interesting: verse 19 concludes with the word "greediness". "The love of money is the root of all evil" (1 Timothy 6:10), and greediness was one of the reasons why the Lord destroyed Sodom and Gomorrah. It wasn't just because of sexual perversion, but greediness and selfishness also played its part in the downfall and ultimate destruction of Sodom and Gomorrah.

VERSES 20-24: "But ye have not so learned Christ; If so be that ye have heard him, and have been taught by him, as the truth is in Jesus: That ye put off concerning the former

conversation the old man, which is corrupt according to the deceitful lusts; And be renewed in the spirit of your mind; And that ye put on the new man, which after God is created in righteousness and true holiness."

Interesting from verse 21: he says you haven't heard Him or been taught by Him, in reference to the Lord Jesus Christ. He doesn't say you saw Him visibly, because you haven't seen Him visibly. "No man hath seen God at any time" (John 1:18), and Jesus makes it very clear how those that had seen Him (Jesus Christ, not God the Father, of course) were blessed. "The just shall live by faith" (Romans 1:17). So, no one living today has seen Jesus Christ in the flesh. Why? Because He is in Heaven. We live by faith, not by sight.

And that's why Paul says, "If so be that ye have heard him [faith comes by hearing], and have been taught by him [and John told us how we have an unction which comes from Heaven and we need not that any man teach us], as the truth is in Jesus: That ye put off concerning the former conversation the old man [in reference to your old nature], which is corrupt [it's dead, it's filthy, it's despicable] according to the deceitful lusts [plural]; And be renewed in the spirit of your mind [read the word of God each and every day!]; And that ye [all of you] put on the new man [the new nature, the seed within you which cannot sin], which after God, is created in righteousness and true holiness", without such, no man shall see God, according to the writer of Hebrews (verse 12:14).

And he's given these warnings time after time because it's possible, if not probable, that Christians that he was writing to were falling back into their old ways. Just look at the church in

Corinth. Look at Ananias and Sapphira, Acts chapter 5. They sinned and the Lord God killed them.

The Corinthians were wilfully sinning, and some were dying because of their sins. And that term "to fall into sin" is too weak. When you sin wilfully against the Lord God of the Bible, that is wilful rebellion.

And when Moses came down from the mount and found many of them sinning, he destroyed 3000 of them in one night. God is holy; He cannot behold evil. So, when you sin against God, you are risking destruction and ultimately damnation. It could be temporary, it could be eternal.

But thankfully, this is not in reference to a person's salvation. These verses (I believe) are pointing to the potential loss of a millennial inheritance for the unrepentant born-again Bible-believer, who has been called a saint and a faithful member of the church in Ephesus - and vicariously in reference to all of us of course - if we have been born-again.

And I'll say this again, if I may, that the born-again Bible believer has two natures: the old nature and the new nature. The new nature cannot sin (according to 1 John chapter 3), but the old nature (according to Romans 7 and Philippians 3) cannot be redeemed. And these two natures clash day in and day out. Hence, why it's imperative for you - the born-again Bible believer - to walk in the Spirit, not in the flesh, to renew your mind each and every day and be careful what you put before your eyes, because your eyes are the windows of your soul.

And if you become lazy and complacent and backslidden and if you fall into sins, and don't repent of those sins, then I think you'll arrive at the Judgment Seat with nothing to await you. If you've fallen from grace, if you are now living in sin, if you are rebelling against God, turn back to Him. Read Luke chapter 15, how the prodigal son ran back to the father and the father ran to him, and the two were reconciled. It broke the father's heart to lose his son, but his son came to himself and when he did so, he went back to his father and his father went to him, and the two were reconciled.

"If we confess our sins, he [God] is faithful and just to forgive us *our* sins, and to cleanse us from all unrighteousness" (1 John 1:9). But, my friend, if you fall from grace, you have to come back to Him. The Lord God is ready and awaiting, arms opened to receive you back into His fold. So, come back to Him, please.

VERSE 25: "Wherefore putting away lying, speak every man truth with his neighbour: for we are members one of another."

Your testimony, if you are saved, should be consistent 24/7. What you do in your local church or fellowship should be done in your communities. What you do at home should be done in your workplace. And he says here: put away lying. The word of God says if we say we have not sinned, we make Him a liar. Christians, my friends, do sin. They shouldn't sin, but they do sin. And when you do sin - when we all sin (and I include myself now) - we confess our sins to God, and He forgives us of our sins straight away. But Paul makes it very clear here: "Speak every man [and woman] truth with his neighbour: for we are members one of another." One Christian fails, it shames another Christian. One Christian falls, it is disgraces another Christian and ultimately the Lord God of the Bible.

Look at verses 26-27, please: **"Be ye angry, and sin not: let not the sun go down upon your wrath: Neither give place to the devil."**

A righteous anger is fine. The Lord Jesus Christ forcibly drove out the moneylenders from the temple more than once. That was a righteous anger, but Paul says: don't sin: "let not the sun go down upon your wrath". Don't become bitter or indifferent or start to brood because something or someone has gone against you during your day.

A failure's crept in. You had high expectations for something to occur. And it didn't happen. Don't let "the sun go down upon your wrath, neither give place to the devil" because he will jump on you the moment he sees that you have lost your fellowship and peace and joy with the Lord. And once he gets into your life, it's very difficult to get him out of your life. So, have a righteous anger, yes. But not an unrighteous anger. Sin not, and don't let "the sun go down upon your wrath." Deal with it as soon as you can. Go to bed with your sins all confessed up. Go to bed in peace and joy through the Holy Ghost, after reading the word of God.

Look at verse 28, please: **"Let him that stole steal no more: but rather let him labour, working with *his* hands the thing which is good, that he may have to give to him that needeth."**

If you can work, you should work. And if you've stolen as a Christian, stop stealing. Turn around, forsake your rebellious ways, and start afresh with the Lord.

VERSE 29: "Let no corrupt communication proceed out of your mouth, but that which is good to the use of edifying, that it may minister grace unto the hearers."

If you're a Christian, what you say should be clean, decent and God-honouring. You should never use four-letter words, and on top of that you should never be gossiping or backbiting or saying something which would dishonour God. Because people hear you (like your neighbours found here in verse 25) and when they hear you blaspheming or cursing or gossiping or backbiting, you blaspheme God and you've lost (temporarily at least) your testimony among them.

And because of this, verse 30 follows: **"And grieve not the holy Spirit of God, whereby ye are sealed unto the day of redemption."**

The Holy Spirit is God. You can grieve Him, you can quench Him and you can dishonour Him, because He lives within you. He sees and hears everything that you do and say.

So, don't grieve Him by filthy communication coming out of your mouth, through stealing (verse 28) or lying (verse 25). So, don't grieve the Holy Spirit of God.

VERSES 31-32: "Let all bitterness, and wrath, and anger, and clamour, and evil speaking, be put away from you, with all malice: And be ye kind one to another, tenderhearted, forgiving one another, even as God for Christ's sake hath forgiven you."

Bitterness, wrath, anger, clamour, evil-speaking: don't let it once be named among you. Put it away from you along with malice, and in its place be tenderhearted, kind to one another, forgiving one another. Why? "Even as God for Christ's sake hath forgiven you."

He's forgiven you totally, so you should be able to forgive those that have wronged you. Otherwise the devil (verse 27) will get a hold on you, and the devil and your flesh coming at you at the same time will cripple you, and you will fall from grace. And that's not what Paul wants for his saints and faithful in Ephesus. And vicariously for those of us living today either.

So, one quick recap from Ephesians chapter 4.

Paul calls himself a prisoner again, demonstrating his humility. And he beseeches those - he begs those - to "walk worthy of the vocation wherewith ye are called." All of us! "With all lowliness and meekness, with long-suffering... to keep the unity of the Spirit in the bond of peace." Why? Because there's one Body - meaning one Church -, one Spirit - meaning the Holy Ghost - "even as ye are called in one hope of your calling; One Lord [Father, Son and Holy Spirit], one faith [Bible-believing Christianity], one baptism [spiritual]" the moment you believed on Him. Not water baptism, but a spiritual baptism which occurred the moment you believed on Him.

"One God and Father of all [only one God in the entire universe; all the others are false deities], who *is* above all, and through all, and in you all [in reference to those which have been born again]."

Verse 7: "Unto every one of us is given grace according to the measure of the gift of Christ." Some people, like I've said, will be missionaries and will die overseas for their faith in the Lord Jesus. Some will be pastors, elders, deacons, perhaps street evangelists maybe. No two people are going to be equipped with the same gift.

In verse 8, he says how Jesus "ascended up on high [third heaven], he led captivity captive [those dead in the ground], and gave gifts [for the Church] unto men." We're all saved the same way, but we are not all equipped to serve Him in the same way.

But before He ascended (verse 9), He descended into the lower parts of the earth (Hell, Hades, Sheol, the Pit, Tartarus, Gehenna). It's all the same place. And He went into the ground to rescue, to redeem, to receive unto Himself the righteous dead that He had died for. And whilst He was there, He preached victory to the unrighteous wicked dead. Those that rejected Him. He proclaimed victory over them (and no doubt the devils as well), how He had been victorious, and how He and He alone had conquered death.

And afterwards (verse 10) "He that descended is the same also that ascended up far above all heavens, that he might fill all things", demonstrating His deity. He can be everywhere at the same time and be all-powerful, proving that Jesus Christ is God Almighty.

In verse 11, He gave some apostles, prophets, evangelists, pastors and teachers (all past tense) and of course, the apostles were eyewitnesses of the Lord Jesus Christ. The prophets were inter-testimonial messengers from law to grace during the time of the compiling of the New Testament. Why? For the perfecting of the saints. And the saints - one more time - is someone who has been born again for the work of the ministry, for the edifying of the Body of Christ.

Now, with the New Testament, we don't need these men in the same way. But saying that, I will say this: that faithful men have always been in existence throughout any given generation to teach the Bible verse by verse, book by book, chapter by chapter, like I'm doing today. But an apostle, a prophet, an evangelist who was able to do supernatural sign gifts is no more. "The just shall <u>live</u> [function] by faith" (Romans 1:17).

And the reason why these men are no longer needed is because we now have the entire New Testament. But the word of God is needed and faithful men are needed to avoid children being tossed to and fro by false doctrine (verse 14) and cunning craftiness, through philosophical means, false teachings.

But speak the truth in love (verse 15) to "grow up into Him in all things, which is the head, *even* Christ." He is the Head of the Body, He is the Head of the church, not the pope and the archbishop of Canterbury. Not an apostle or prophet or bishop or deacon or a reverend.

Jesus Christ is the Head of His own Church, and Paul - as a loving spiritual father - reaffirms the warning from verses 17 down to 32 to <u>walk</u> in the Spirit. Don't follow the unbelieving Gentiles or Jews, who walk in darkness, who follow the vanity of their mind - the science religion known as evolution, perhaps, or philosophy in general - having their understanding darkened [blurred].

Verse 18: "being alienated from the life of God through the ignorance that is in them, because of the blindness of their heart". He's saying: don't follow them. It's possible you could follow them. I love you. It'll break my heart if you follow them and never got out of that snare.

"Who being past feeling [verse 19] have given themselves over unto lasciviousness." You are your own worst enemy, if you're not saved. And even if you are saved, you are still your own worst enemy. What happens? "To work all uncleanness with greediness." "The love of money is the root of all evil." "But ye [all of you] have not so learned Christ [He lives inside or us and teaches us]; If so be that you have heard him, and have been taught by him, as the truth is in Jesus." It's possible some of these people weren't even saved; hence, why he is saying this.

But in verse 22, he continues on: "That ye [all of you] put off concerning the former conversation the old man which is corrupt [it's dying!] according to the deceitful lusts; And be renewed in the spirit of your mind." How? By reading the word of God, walking in the spirit - not the flesh - "And that ye put on the new man, which after God is created in righteousness and true holiness."

The burden is on you, my friends, to walk in the Spirit, to put on the new man. Jesus Christ saved you and He will keep you saved (chapter 4, verse 30), but you are expected to walk in holiness and obey Him. He won't do everything for you. He expects you to do that yourselves. Protect your testimonies around your neighbours (verse 25) and stop lying. "Be ye angry" with a righteous anger. Hate sin, hate heresies, hate false teachings, hate your own sin nature and sin not.

"Let not the sun go down upon your wrath." Don't go to bed feeling angry or bitter or twisted. Deal with it. Why? Because if you don't, you'll give place to the devil (verse 27).

Verse 28: "Let him that stole steal no more: but rather let him labour, working with *his* hands the thing which is good, that he may have to give to him that needeth." You don't work, you don't eat. And once again, this goes back to your testimony, your standing in the eyes of your neighbours (verse 25).

Verse 29: No cursing should come from your mouths, no gossiping, no backbiting, no filthy talk, no foolish talking, no jesting and no sexual innuendos. "Grieve not the Holy Spirit... whereby ye are sealed unto the day of redemption." "Once saved, always saved; or if saved, always saved" is a true Biblical doctrine, but along the way, don't grieve the Holy Ghost.

And verse 31 down to 32: "Let all bitterness, and wrath, and anger, and clamour, and evil speaking, be put away from you, with all malice: And be ye kind one to another, tenderhearted, forgiving one another [without exception, do it straight away, don't hold a grudge] even as God for Christ's sake hath forgiven you."

He did everything for us on the cross, and He expects us to do as much as we can for Him and the brethren.

CHAPTER 5

VERSES 1-2: "Be ye therefore followers of God, as dear children; And walk in love, as Christ also hath loved us, and hath given himself for us an offering and a sacrifice to God for a sweetsmelling savour."

Paul said to: follow me as I follow Christ. Now he says: follow God as dear children. Jesus told Thomas he that seeth the Son, seeth the Father. So, you want a good role model in your life? Follow the Lord Jesus Christ.

VERSES 3-4: "But fornication, and all uncleanness, or covetousness, let it not be once named among you, as becometh saints; Neither filthiness, nor foolish talking, nor jesting, which are not convenient: but rather giving of thanks."

Don't even let it be named once among you (verse two) in reference to fornication - *pornea* in Greek - which deals with every sexual sin imaginable or all uncleanness or covetousness. 'I want this, I want that.' He says: forget it, don't even let it be once be named among you. The word of God tells us if you think about something sinful long enough, you've already done it, meaning to lust after a woman or to lust after a man is the same as committing adultery. Just think it and you've done it.

But Paul goes beyond that. He says: don't even let these sins be named among you. In fact, he's moving on from the last chapter - dealing with lying, stealing, and unrighteous anger - to now sins of the flesh, real sexual sins of the flesh. And he's leading up to one's millennial inheritance (verse 5) and he says in verse 4, "Neither filthiness, nor foolish talking, nor jesting, which are not convenient [meaning it's not acceptable]: but rather giving of thanks." Filthiness, sexual innuendos, wicked talking, filthy talking, implying, suggesting, playing the fool - he says no, "but rather giving of thanks."

In fact, the Lord Jesus said the following in Matthew 12:36: "But I say unto you, That every idle word that men shall speak, they shall give account thereof in the day of judgment. For by thy words thou shalt be justified, and by thy words thou shalt be condemned."

He sees and hears everything, so be careful what you say because one day He will call you to account, and all your filthiness, all your foolish talking and jesting will be replayed in the presence of the Father, the Son, the Holy Ghost and His angels.

But look at Ephesians 5:5, please: **"For this ye know, that no whoremonger, nor unclean person, nor covetous man, who is an idolater, hath any inheritance in the kingdom of Christ and of God."**

This would be in reference to the Millennial Kingdom. A whoremonger would be a man or a woman who is perpetually promiscuous, who sleeps around. An unclean person would deal with all sexual immorality, and a covetous man is someone who cannot stop lusting, which feeds into idolatry. Not just in reference to worshipping false deities but worshipping yourself, worshipping your wife or your girlfriend or your boyfriend or your husband. And he says these people have no inheritance in the Kingdom of Christ and of God.

And yet while on the one hand, this verse can be cited to show unsaved people why they will not go to Heaven when they die, but at the same time, I think Paul is speaking to Christians who comit these sins (found verse 5), they don't repent of such sins, and they go on to forfeit their right to inherit the Kingdom of God, the thousand-year reign, of course.

And like I said in verse 3, fornication is *pornea* in Greek and that covers everything from bestiality to incest to sodomy to lesbianism, adultery and all kinds of infidelity. And these people, according to the word of God, that persist in such sins, that never repent of their rebellious nature, will have no part in the inheritance of the Kingdom of Christ and of God. Pure and simple! If you live after the flesh (if you're saved), this is what will occur. And if you're not saved and you're living left, right and centre, hellfire awaits you when you die.

VERSE 6: "Let no man deceive you with vain words: for because of these things cometh the wrath of God upon the children of disobedience."

Don't listen to liberal apostates. Go to the word of God, read it for yourselves. There are too many people out there who are going around saying: "God loves everyone. Live as you will and you'll go to Heaven when you die." These are vain words. They are adherents of hyper grace. This is foolish talking, found in verse 4. Lying, found in chapter 4, verse 25. And even stealing, chapter 4 verse 28. Because you're stealing God of His Holiness and His righteousness and because of these things, the wrath of God, the anger of God, comes upon the children of disobedience, in reference to unsaved people and also quite possibly in reference to backslidden, rebellious and carnal Christians who are now going about telling people they can live as they will and there's no consequences for their sins. They have fallen so far from grace that it's just so tragic.

And Paul says in verse 7: **"Be not ye therefore partakers with them."**

Separation. Mark them out, warn others and then separate from them.

VERSES 8-10: "For ye were sometimes darkness, but now *are ye* light in the Lord: walk as children of light: (For the fruit of the Spirit *is* in all goodness and righteousness and truth;) Proving what is acceptable unto the Lord."

Check someone out in light of Holy Scripture. A person tells you this or a person tells you that. Go to the Scripture and check them out. Judge them with righteous judgment (chapter 4, verse 26).

Look at verse 11, please: **"And have no fellowship with the unfruitful works of darkness, but rather reprove *them*."**

Rebuke them sharply. Don't even fellowship with them. Don't associate with them. Don't socialise with them. Why? Verse 12: **"For it is a shame even to speak of those things which are done of them in secret."**

When I read this verse, I almost think of the Freemasons, who meet in secret and blaspheme the one true God. They call him Jahbulon, taking the first three letters for Jehovah or Yahweh and adding Ba'al and Osiris to complete this wicked name. But God is not called Jahbulon. He's called Jehovah, Yahweh, Adonai, Lord or Father. And these things are done in secret, and Paul says it is even a shame, a disgrace to even speak of such things.

But look at verse 13: **"But all things that are reproved are made manifest by the light: for whatsoever doth make manifest is light."**

And yet Jesus told us how men loved darkness rather than light. Why? Because their deeds were evil. There's enough light in the world to save mankind, but mankind has to come voluntarily unto the Author of light. And if you don't come, you won't be saved. And if you die unsaved, you'll go to Hell when you die and being in Hell, you'll have only yourself to blame.

But look at verse 14, please: **"Wherefore he saith, Awake thou that sleepest, and arise from the dead, and Christ shall give thee light."**

It's almost a call to be saved. It's almost a call for the backslidden to come back and walk with the Lord Jesus Christ.

VERSES 15-16: "See then that ye walk circumspectly, not as fools, but as wise, Redeeming the time, because the days are evil."

There's not much you can do with a secular, agnostic and indifferent generation, but you can redeem the days. Get some tracts, get a sign. Go onto the streets. Go door to door. Speak to people: friends, family, neighbours, work colleagues. Tell them about the Lord Jesus Christ. Redeem the time, because the days are evil!

VERSE 17: "Wherefore be ye not unwise, but understanding what the will of the Lord *is*."

If you want to know the will of the Lord in your life, go to the word of God. It's as simple as that.

VERSES 18-21: "And be not drunk with wine, wherein is excess; but be filled with the Spirit; Speaking to yourselves in psalms and hymns and spiritual songs, singing and making melody in your heart to the Lord; Giving thanks always for all things unto God and the Father in the name of our Lord

Jesus Christ; Submitting yourselves one to another in the fear of God."

Verse 19: "Speaking to yourselves in psalms and hymns and spiritual songs." Be very careful as to what type of music you listen to. Some music is inappropriate for a Christian. Some music is laden with explicit, ungodly and even satanic lyrics. And some music has even been produced by witches and Satanists.

Verse 20: "Giving thanks always for all things unto God and the Father in the name of our Lord Jesus Christ;" and verse 21: "Submitting yourselves one to another in the fear of God." He that is greatest among you, let him be as your servant. So, no one should be arrogant enough to think they know everything. And no one should be of the mindset that they cannot be taught anything from anyone else other than themselves.

VERSE 22: "Wives, submit yourselves unto your own husbands, as unto the Lord."

This would be in reference to a saved wife submitting herself to her saved husband. For saved wives living with unsaved husbands, it's a little different: you should be a living epistle. But here the apostle Paul is speaking to saved wives submitting themselves to their saved husbands. Why?

VERSES 23-24: "For the husband is the head of the wife, even as Christ is the head of the church: and he is the saviour of the body. Therefore as the church is subject unto Christ, so *let* the wives *be* to their own husbands in every thing."

A saved wife submits to her saved husband as her saved husband submits to Christ, who is the Head of the Church and He is the Saviour of the Body. And now Paul will deal with husbands.

VERSES 25-27: "Husbands, love your wives, even as Christ also loved the church, and gave himself for it; That he might sanctify and cleanse it with the washing of water by the word, That he might present it to himself a glorious church, not having spot, or wrinkle, or any such thing; but that it should be holy and without blemish."

This is imputed righteousness, of course. Only through His divine blood can He present His church to Himself spotless, wrinkle-free and without blemish. And also from verse 25, Christ also loved the Church and gave Himself for it. He died for the sins of the world, but here Paul is speaking about those which have appropriated the atonement.

Verse 26: "That he might sanctify [bless it, set it apart] and cleanse it with the washing of water [not literal water, of course; this is symbolic of His precious blood] by the word, That he might present it to himself a glorious church." Only through His precious blood, as I say. Man in his best state is altogether vanity.

And the latter part of verse 27, "that it [the Church] should be holy", meaning "set apart and covered", one final time, by His own precious and divine blood.

Look at verses 28-30: **"So ought men to love their wives as their own bodies. He that loveth his wife loveth himself. For no man ever yet hated his own flesh; but nourisheth and cherisheth it, even as the Lord the church: For we are members of his body, of his flesh, and of his bones."**

It's common sense, really. A man should love his wife as he loves his own body. Why? Because we are members of His body, being the Church, which is His flesh and His bones. It's a picture of Adam and Eve, of course.

But he continues to move on.

Look at verse 31: **"For this cause shall a man leave his father and mother, and shall be joined unto his wife, and they two shall be one flesh."**

This, of course, is marriage, not cohabitation. A man meets a woman and they get married, and they go on to produce a child. Holy matrimony! A man with a man and a woman with a woman is simply unknown in the eyes of the Lord.

VERSE 32: "This is a great mystery: but I speak concerning Christ and the church."

A mystery, meaning something which was kept secret for a period of time, but now has been revealed to the apostle Paul. Paul is the apostle to the Gentiles, whereas Simon Peter was the apostle to the Jews. But this mystery, in essence, dealt with how we are all in the Body of Christ. The Holy Spirit puts us (Jew and Gentile, male and female) into the Body of Christ, something which had been unknown pre-the New Covenant.

But now Paul had been entrusted to explain this to the Ephesians, the Corinthians, the Philippians and all of the churches for which he was responsible for.

VERSE 33: "Nevertheless let every one of you in particular so love his wife even as himself; and the wife see that she reverence *her* husband."

Sarah revered Abraham, and a saved woman should revere her husband as her husband reveres Jesus Christ, who is the Head of the Church, of course.

So, to recap chapter 5.

Verse 1: "Be ye therefore followers of God, as dear children." Follow Him, even when it costs you something. "Walk in love" because Christ has loved us and given Himself for us as "an offering and a sacrifice to God for a sweetsmelling savour." But fornication - *pornea*, all sexual illicit sins - don't let it once be "named among you, as becometh saints. Neither filthiness nor foolish talking nor jesting, which are not convenient: but rather giving of thanks." Be careful what you say (in verse 4) and what you do (in verse 3).

And in case there's any confusion, in verse 5: "this ye know, that no warmonger, nor unclean person, nor covetous man, who is an idolater, hath any inheritance in the kingdom of Christ and of God. If you persist in sins - found here - the kingdom of God is not for you when you die. You will lose your millennial inheritance, not your salvation, but your right to rule and reign with Him for a thousand years.

And he says in verse 6 "Let no man deceive you with vain words." Be careful who you listen to. Philosophy will take you further away from God. And because Paul knows that people are going to come along and teach sin being acceptable, he says, "Let no man deceive you with vain words [verse 6] for because of these things cometh the wrath of God upon the children of disobedience."

Don't listen to these people. They're liars, they're fakes, they're charlatans. "Be not ye therefore partakers with them" (verse 7) because if you do, you too will be chastised and possibly condemned along with them, and he even says in verse 8, "For ye were [past tense] sometimes darkness, but now [present tense] *are ye* light in the Lord: walk as children of light [back to verse 1 again] (For the fruit of the Spirit *is* in all goodness and righteousness and truth;) Proving what is acceptable unto the Lord."

Go to the word of God. Check people out. It's as simple as that. Verse 11 down to 13: Don't have any fellowship with such people. It's even a shame to talk about what they do, but reprove them, expose them and then turn from them.

Verse 14 down to 16: if you're backslidden: "Awake thou that sleepest, and arise from the dead." Why? So that "Christ can give thee light" in reference to one being saved and also in reference to coming back into the light of Christ.

Do you want to do something constructive for the Lord (verse 16)? Redeem the time. Why? Because the days are evil. Do something constructive for your Father.

And verses 18 down to 20 speak about people having joy and power and peace with the Lord, and that comes through hymns, psalms and spiritual songs and "Giving thanks always for all things unto God and the Father in the name of our Lord Jesus Christ, submitting yourselves one to another [verse 21] in the fear of God" which teaches humility, of course. And also from verse 21, this deals with accountability one to another.

Verses 22 down to 33 deals with saved wives and their saved husbands. And they are to submit to one another because the man is the head of the family and Christ is the Head of the Church. And this is done primarily from verse 27: "That he [Jesus] might present it to himself a glorious church, not having spot, or wrinkle, or any such thing; but that it should be holy and without blemish." And He can do that and He has done that, but Paul is also wanting Christians to realise that their testimonies and their lifestyles will have consequences for them, if they don't repent and turn from that.

So, as always, there's many themes in Paul's epistles: salvation on the one hand, service on the other hand; Heaven on the one hand, the millennial kingdom on the other hand.

In verse 31, He upholds marriage: one man, one woman, period.

CHAPTER 6

VERSES 1-3: "Children, obey your parents in the Lord: for this is right. Honour thy father and mother; (which is the first commandment with promise;) That it may be well with thee, and thou mayest live long on the earth."

Chapter 6 commences with Paul speaking to saved children submitting themselves to their saved parents. Why? That "thou mayest live long on the earth." In the Old Testament, disobedience to parents resulted in death. In the New Covenant, disobedience to parents could result in dying prematurely.

Chapter 6, verse 4: "And, ye fathers, provoke not your children to wrath: but bring them up in the nurture and admonition of the Lord."

Now he's switching it to fathers: don't provoke your children to wrath. Children watch their parents like a hawk. So, practice what you preach, and preach what you practice.

VERSES 5-8: "Servants, be obedient to them that are *your* masters according to the flesh, with fear and trembling, in singleness of your heart, as unto Christ; Not with eyeservice, as menpleasers; but as the servants of Christ, doing the will of God from the heart; With good will doing service, as to the Lord, and not to men: Knowing that whatsoever good thing any man doeth, the same shall he receive of the Lord, whether *he be* bond or free."

Don't sit around, servants (which for today would be employees), if your masters are saved, waiting for the clock to strike five. Do a good day's work and even if your employers are not saved, do a good days work. Why? Because you serve Christ Jesus our Lord.

VERSE 9: "And, ye masters, do the same things unto them, forbearing threatening: knowing that your Master also is in heaven; neither is there respect of persons with him."

Now the switch goes to the employer! You have a Master in Heaven. Serve Him too faithfully, so don't mistreat your employees.

VERSES 10-12: "Finally, my brethren, be strong in the Lord, and in the power of his might. Put on the whole armour of God, that ye may be able to stand against the wiles of the devil. For we wrestle not against flesh and blood, but against principalities, against powers, against the rulers of the darkness of this world, against spiritual wickedness in high *places*."

Behind each of the last chapters, he dealt with the problem of the flesh and Satan as well. But in chapter 6, he's focusing primarily on Satan from verses 11 down to verses 24 because he ultimately is the enemy of the brethren.

Yes, your flesh is your number one enemy, but Satan is ultimately your enemy. And his purpose and mission in life is to destroy you at each and every given chance and opportunity. And that's why Paul tells you to "Put on the whole armour of God, that ye [all of you] may be able to stand against the wiles of the devil." It's not enough just to be on the defensive. You have to go on the offensive, like a soldier would have to go into battle to defeat his or her enemy. And here, the analogy is going to be of a professional soldier preparing for a hard and prolonged battle.

But he says in verse 12 how we don't wrestle against flesh and blood, meaning we don't go out to fight people physically, but we wrestle "against principalities [the invisible angelic world], against powers [perhaps false teachers, or more likely the spirits which control them], against the rulers of the darkness of this world, against spiritual wickedness in high *places*." Satan is the prince of the air.

You were told also in Romans to submit to "the powers that be" (Romans 13:1), but the problem is, of course, that the powers that be - although ordained of God - are many times controlled by the powers of darkness. So how are you - the Bible-believing Christian - expected to fight against such powers?

Look at verse 13: **"Wherefore take unto you the whole armour of God, that ye may be able to withstand in the evil day, and having done all, to stand."**

Although the day is spoken of in the singular, I believe it is in reference to each and every day of our lives. And yet soldiers do not fight major battles daily, so the day can also be in reference to when a sudden attack is launched against the saint. And when it comes, stand. Stand firm.

VERSES 14-16: "Stand therefore, having your loins girt about with truth, and having on the breastplate of righteousness; And your feet shod with the preparation of the gospel of peace; Above all, taking the shield of faith, wherewith ye shall be able to quench all the fiery darts of the wicked."

Temptation, trials and tribulations: the devil is behind it all. He's not just going to come at you in the physical way; he will come at you in the spiritual way. He will try to get you not just through unsaved friends and family, but sometimes through saved people as well. He will also try to get you to stop trusting God and the Bible for help, but the flesh and people.

VERSES 17-20: "And take the helmet of salvation, and the sword of the Spirit, which is the word of God: Praying always with all prayer and supplication in the Spirit, and watching thereunto with all perseverance and supplication for all saints; And for me, that utterance may be given unto me, that I may open my mouth boldly, to make known the mystery of the gospel, For which I am an ambassador in bonds: that therein I may speak boldly, as I ought to speak."

Paul's not concerned about his own physical welfare. He's more concerned about speaking the gospel boldly to those that will listen to him. And once again, he sets the bar when it comes to true Christian living.

But the key to these verses is found in verses 17 and 18: "And take the helmet of salvation, and the sword of the Spirit, which is the word of God: Praying always [without exception] with all prayer and supplication in the Spirit, and watching thereunto with all perseverance and supplication for all saints." You see, you were told to love the brethren, so now you are not only fighting the devil in a spiritual sense for your own sake, you're fighting him also for the saints.

But he says in verse 20 how he is "an ambassador in bonds". Hence, why he calls himself a prisoner "that therein I may speak boldly, as I ought to speak." Remarkable! This man faced death almost every day of his life. He wasn't bothered about dying. He was more bothered about not giving the gospel out to those that he would meet on his travels. "Woe is unto me if I preach not the gospel" (1 Corinthians 9:16).

But look at verses 21-22, please: **"But that ye also may know my affairs, and how I do, Tychicus, a beloved brother and faithful minister in the Lord, shall make known to you all things: Whom I have sent unto you for the same purpose, that ye might know our affairs, and that he might comfort your hearts."**

Tychicus would hand deliver this epistle to the Ephesians and then report back to Paul with news from this church. Paul may also have dictated this epistle to Tychicus due to his eyesight only getting worse. And note, nobody was able to heal Paul. The Jewish sign gifts are receding.

VERSE 23: "Peace be to the brethren, and love with faith, from God the Father and the Lord Jesus Christ.

But he has to sign off his epistle with peace, faith and love from God the Father and the Lord Jesus Christ.

VERSE 24: "Grace be with all them that love our Lord Jesus Christ in sincerity. Amen."

And that's the key: to love Him in sincerity, to have your heart circumcised. Not a head knowledge but a true heartfelt love for Him, obedience to him and a sincere desire to grow in grace. And that word "grace" was found in the first chapter, verse 2, and it concludes chapter 6, verse 24.

But the final word is "Amen", "so may it be", meaning everything that Paul had told us in this epistle was now to be commended back to the Lord God of the Bible.

So, to recap chapter 6, if we may, children are told to submit to their parents if they wish to live long on the earth. Fathers are told not to provoke their children to wrath, but to practice what they preach and to preach what they practice. Servants are told to honour their masters, not just for the master's sake, but for the

Lord Jesus Christ's sake. And the same also goes for the masters, because they serve one Master who is in Heaven.

And in verses 11 down to 16, the Christian is pictured as a soldier, not preparing for physical battle of course, but for spiritual battle. And he/she can overcome the devil's fiery darts when he walks in the Holy Spirit, when he prays with all supplication, when he uses the word of God to defeat heresies and heretics and all false teachings. There is no such thing as a Christian consciences objector.

And Paul once again - ever the humble Christian - credits Tychicus, the brother who wrote this epistles as Paul dictated it to him. But Paul doesn't want people to be overloaded with fear and worry and he closes his epistle in verse 23 with the word "peace" and in verse 24 with the word "Amen."

But between verses 23 and 24, he speaks about the love of God and how this epistle ultimately is for those that love Him in sincerity. So, if you love God in sincerity, He loves you as well. Amen.

But please keep in mind that if you are born-again Bible-believing Christian, you will always need to be on your guard because Satan goes around like a roaring lion seeking to devour whom he will. And yet God has given you the power the ability to quench all the fiery darts of the devil: prayer, fasting, Scripture and obedience to God.

And one final thought from me in reference to verse 19: "that utterance may be given unto me, that I may open my mouth boldly, to make known the mystery of the gospel."

The apostle Paul was a soul winner and he told us to be ready in season and out of season when it came to witnessing to people, to being faithful ambassadors for Christ. In fact, this

Scripture almost mirrors chapter 5, verse 16: "Redeeming the time, because the days are evil."

Paul told us how he went to the third heaven how he had perfect knowledge of all things, and yet according to Calvinists, God has already chosen His elect before the foundation of the world. But that's not what Paul tells us: please pray for me, he says, "that utterance may be given unto me, that I may open my mouth boldly, to make known the mystery of the gospel." Why bother, Paul? If the elect have already been chosen, surely you would have known this? But he says no. "For which I am an ambassador in bonds: that therein I may speak boldly, as I ought to speak." He was a soul winner and he told us from 1 Corinthians to follow him as he follows Christ. So, we too should be soul winners as and when we possibly can, but above all we should be Bereans and we should be presenting our bodies daily to the Lord as living sacrifices.

And on that note I shall conclude this unscripted verse-by-verse Bible study through the Epistle to the Ephesians, and I hope you all began with me and you finished with me, and above all that you had your Bibles opened and you're reading along with me as I took you through six chapters of the Epistle to the Ephesians.

The Lord bless you all in Jesus name. Amen and amen!

Also by James Battell

The Shocking History of the Jesuits (The Society of Jesus)
King James I of England: The King The Vatican Could Not Kill
The Hidden Truth About Freemasonry, The Catholic Church,
And The Illuminati
Bible Prophecy Made Simple For Serious Students of Scripture
Did The Catholic Church Order Abraham Lincoln's
Assassination?
Is Calvinism and the Doctrines of Grace Biblical?
The Book of Genesis Commentary (Chapters 1-11)
The Book of Genesis Commentary (Chapters 1-11)
Watchman Nee, Witness Lee, and Living Stream Ministry: A
Critical Analysis of Their Identity as Cult or Church
What Is Speaking In Tongues And Is It Still For Today?
Ephesians KJV Bible Commentary
The Book of Romans Commentary
Philemon Bible Study (Slavery In Scripture)
Turbulent Thrones: Charles vs. Cromwell's Epic Struggle for
England's Soul
The Holy Ghost Within The Trinity
Papal Infallibility or Insanity?
The Immaculate Conception ("Deception")